Binary Options

Adrienne Morel

Adrienne Morel

Adrienne Morel

Copyright Page

Index

Introduction to Binary Options

The world of trading is full of opportunities for those who want to invest and make profits in the financial markets. One of the most popular and accessible ways to trade is through binary options. Although the name may sound complicated, in reality, binary options are a fairly simple form of investment that anyone, with the right knowledge, can understand and use.

Binary options, also known as digital or fixed-return options, are a type of financial instrument that allows traders to speculate on the future direction of an asset. In simple terms, when you trade binary options, you only have two possible outcomes: you either win a fixed amount of money or you lose your initial investment. This is where the name "binary" comes from, as there are only two possible outcomes. This makes them especially attractive to new traders looking for simplicity and clarity in their investments.

To begin understanding binary options, we must first discuss the basic components of a binary trade. First, you need to select an underlying asset. This asset can be a stock, a currency pair, a commodity such as gold or oil, or even a stock index. Once you have chosen the asset, you must predict whether its price will rise or fall within a given time period. This time period, known as the expiration time, can vary from a few minutes to several days.

Imagine that you are interested in trading the stock of a well-known company, such as Apple. If you think that the price of Apple's stock will rise in the next hour, you can buy a "buy" or "call" binary option. If your prediction is correct and the price of Apple's stock does indeed rise at the end of that hour, you will earn a fixed amount of money, pre-specified by the broker. On the other hand, if you think that the price of Apple's stock will fall in the next hour, you can buy a "sell" or "put" binary option. If the price of the stock falls at the end of the time period, you will earn a fixed amount. However, if your prediction is wrong, you will lose your initial investment.

The history of binary options is relatively recent in the financial world. Although the concepts behind these options have been around for a long time, it was only from the 2000s that binary options started gaining popularity among retail traders. The main reason for their rapid growth is the simplicity and transparency they offer. Unlike other forms of trading, where profits and losses can be difficult to calculate due to market fluctuations, binary options offer absolute clarity on how much you can win or lose before you place a trade.

Despite their advantages, binary options also have disadvantages. The main one is the risk of losing your entire initial investment in a single trade if your prediction is wrong. Also, due to the binary nature of these options, payouts are usually lower compared to other forms of trading. This means that while you can make money quickly, you can also lose money quickly if you don't have a solid strategy and good risk management.

Binary options are traded through online trading platforms, offered by a variety of brokers. Choosing the right broker is crucial to a successful trading experience. It is important to do your research and select a broker that is regulated and has a good reputation in the industry. Modern trading platforms offer a variety of tools and resources to help traders make informed decisions, including charts, technical indicators, and market analysis.

One of the most appealing aspects of binary options is their accessibility. You don't need to be a financial expert to start trading. With a relatively low initial investment and an easy-to-use trading platform, virtually anyone can begin exploring the world of binary options trading. However, it's important to remember that while the trading process may be simple, success in this field requires learning, practice, and discipline.

In short, binary options are an exciting and accessible way to invest in the financial markets. They offer a simple way to speculate on the price direction of various assets, with the potential for fixed, known profits in advance. However, they also come with risks, and it is crucial to approach binary options trading with a learning mindset and careful risk management. As we progress through this book, we will explore in detail the strategies and techniques that can help you maximize your profits and minimize your losses in the world of binary options trading.

Understanding the Binary Options Market

The binary options market can seem intimidating at first, but once you understand its fundamentals, it becomes much more manageable and even exciting. This chapter will guide you through the essentials of the binary options market, from option types to underlying assets, market hours and volatility. With a little patience and attention, you will soon feel more comfortable navigating this dynamic investment environment.

First, it is important to know the different types of binary options available to traders. The most common binary options are call options and put options. A call option allows you to bet that the price of an asset will rise in a given time period, while a put option allows you to bet that the price will fall. However, there are other types of binary options that can offer you different opportunities. For example, one touch options allow you to make money if the asset price hits a predetermined level at least once before expiration. No touch options work in reverse: you win if the price never touches the predetermined level. There are also range options, where you bet that the asset price will stay within a specific range for the set time period.

Another key component of the binary options market is the underlying assets. These are the financial instruments on which your options are based. Underlying assets can include a wide variety of instruments, such as stocks, currency pairs, commodities, and stock indices. Stocks represent a stake in a company, and their value can be affected by a variety of factors, such as the company's financial results or market conditions. Currency pairs, such as the Euro/Dollar (EUR/USD), are popular in the binary options market, and their value depends on fluctuations in the exchange rate between two currencies. Commodities, such as gold, oil, or coffee, are also common options, and their price can be influenced by factors such as global supply and demand. Finally, stock indices, which group the stocks of several companies into a single indicator, can provide a broader view of the performance of the market as a whole.

Understanding market hours is crucial to successful binary options trading. Unlike other financial markets that may have limited hours, the binary options market is available 24 hours a day, five days a week. This is because underlying assets, such as currency pairs and commodities, are traded on global markets that are open at different times of the day. For example, the forex market is active 24 hours a day, starting with the Asian session, followed by Europe and then America. This allows you to choose the most convenient times to trade based on your schedule and preference. However, it is important to note that market volatility can vary depending on the time of day. Volatility refers to the amount of movement in the price of an asset. In general, markets tend to be more volatile during the opening of major trading sessions, such as London and New York, which can offer more trading opportunities but also carries more risk.

Market volatility is a critical factor that can influence the success of your trading. In simple terms, volatility measures how quickly and by how much the price of an asset changes over a period of time. Markets with high volatility can offer greater profit opportunities as prices move faster and faster. However, they can also be riskier as prices can change direction abruptly. On the other hand, markets with low volatility tend to be more stable, which can be ideal for more conservative trading strategies. It is important to develop a solid understanding of market volatility and how it affects different underlying assets in order to make informed trading decisions.

In short, understanding the binary options market involves becoming familiar with the different types of options available, the underlying assets, market hours, and volatility. Each of these elements plays a crucial role in the trading process and can influence your decisions and results. By knowing and understanding these fundamentals, you will be better prepared to navigate the exciting world of binary options trading and take advantage of the opportunities it offers. As you continue to learn and practice, you will become more confident and able to make informed and strategic trading decisions.

Trading Platforms and Tools

Success in binary options trading depends not only on your knowledge and strategies, but also on the platforms and tools you use. These tools can make the difference between a smooth and effective trading experience and one filled with frustration and mistakes. In this chapter, we will explore the different trading platforms available and the essential tools that will help you make informed decisions and improve your binary options trading results.

Trading platforms are the medium through which you conduct your trading in the binary options market. Choosing a suitable platform is crucial as it should be reliable, easy to use, and offer the functionalities you need to implement your trading strategies. There are numerous trading platforms on the market, each with its own features and advantages. Some of the most popular ones include MetaTrader 4, MetaTrader 5, and proprietary platforms developed by specific brokers.

MetaTrader 4 (MT4) and MetaTrader 5 (MT5) are widely recognized platforms in the trading world due to their versatility and robustness.

Although they were originally designed for forex trading, they also support binary options. MT4 is known for its user-friendly interface and the availability of numerous technical indicators and analysis tools. On the other hand, MT5 offers additional functionalities, such as more time frames and order types, making it suitable for more advanced traders.

In addition to generic platforms such as MT4 and MT5, many binary options brokers develop their own proprietary platforms. These platforms are usually designed specifically for binary options trading, offering an intuitive and easy-to-navigate interface. When choosing a proprietary platform, it is important to ensure that the broker is regulated and has a good reputation in the industry. This ensures that your funds are safe and that the platform operates in a transparent and fair manner.

Once you have chosen a trading platform, it is time to familiarize yourself with the available tools and resources that can help you make informed decisions. One of the most important tools is price charts. Charts allow you to visualize the historical and current price behavior of an asset, which is essential for performing technical analysis. Charts can be presented in different forms, such as lines, bars, or Japanese candlesticks. Each type of chart has its own advantages and can offer different perspectives on price movement.

Along with price charts, technical indicators are essential tools for analyzing the market and predicting future price movements. Technical indicators are calculations based on the price, volume, or open interest of an asset and are presented as overlaid charts on the price chart. Some of the most commonly used technical indicators in binary options trading include moving averages, relative strength index (RSI), stochastic oscillator, and Bollinger bands. Each of these indicators provides valuable information about the market trend, trend strength, and potential reversal points.

In addition to technical charts and indicators, fundamental analysis tools can also be useful in binary options trading. Fundamental analysis focuses on evaluating economic, financial, and other qualitative factors that can influence the price of an asset. For example, economic data such as interest rates, employment reports, and corporate earnings reports can have a significant impact on the price of underlying assets. Staying informed about economic news and global events is crucial to making informed trading decisions.

Trading signals are another valuable tool that can help you improve your binary options trading results. Trading signals are recommendations generated by expert analysts or automated algorithms that suggest when to buy or sell an asset. These signals are based on technical and fundamental analysis and can help you identify trading opportunities that you might otherwise overlook. However, it is important to remember that trading signals do not guarantee success and should be used as a complementary tool to your own analysis and strategy.

In addition to these analytical tools, modern trading platforms often offer other useful features, such as the ability to perform automated trading via trading robots or custom scripts. Automated trading allows you to automatically execute trades based on predefined rules that you set up. This can be especially useful if you have a specific trading strategy that you want to implement consistently without manual intervention. However, it is important to test and fine-tune any automated strategy on a demo account before using it with real money to ensure that it works as you expect.

In short, trading platforms and tools are essential components for success in binary options trading. Choosing the right platform and familiarizing yourself with the various analysis tools can significantly improve your trading decisions and ultimately your results. As you explore and use these tools, you will develop a deeper understanding of the market and feel more confident in making informed trading decisions. Always remember to keep up to date with the latest trends and technologies in the trading world to keep improving and adapting to changing market conditions.

Basic Strategies for Beginners

Getting into the world of binary options trading can be exciting, but it can also be challenging if you don't have a proper strategy. Having a well-defined trading strategy is essential to increase your chances of success and minimize risks. In this chapter, I will introduce you to some basic strategies for beginners, designed to help you better understand the market and make more informed trading decisions.

One of the simplest and most popular strategies among beginners is the trend-following strategy. This strategy is based on the premise that asset prices tend to move in trends. A trend can be bullish, when prices are rising, or bearish, when prices are falling. The main idea behind this strategy is to "go with the flow" of the market. If you identify an uptrend, you will look for opportunities to buy call options. If you identify a downtrend, you will look for opportunities to buy put options. To identify trends, you can use tools such as moving averages, which smooth out price data and help you see the general direction of the market. A simple moving average (SMA) or exponential moving average (EMA) are good options to start with.

Another basic strategy is the breakout strategy. This strategy focuses on identifying key support and resistance levels on the price chart. Support is a level where prices tend to stop and reverse their direction upward, while resistance is a level where prices tend to stop and reverse their direction downward. When the price breaks a support or resistance level, it can be a sign that a new trend is forming. The breakout strategy involves waiting for the price to break a key level and then entering a trade in the direction of the breakout. For example, if the price breaks a resistance and continues to rise, you might buy a call option. If the price breaks a support and continues to fall, you might buy a put option.

The double investment strategy is another simple technique that can be useful for beginners. This strategy is based on doubling your investment on the next trade if your previous trade resulted in a loss. The idea is that you will eventually win a trade and recover your previous losses along with a profit. However, it is important to note that this strategy can be risky, as a series of consecutive losses can result in a significant loss of capital. Therefore, it is crucial to set clear limits and not risk more than you are willing to lose.

The 60-second strategy is a popular choice among traders who prefer fast and dynamic trading. This strategy involves placing trades with very short expiry times, usually 60 seconds. The key to being successful with this strategy is to quickly identify trading opportunities and act quickly. You can use technical indicators such as the RSI (relative strength index) or the stochastic oscillator to identify overbought or oversold conditions in the market. If the RSI shows that an asset is overbought, you might consider buying a put option, expecting the price to fall in the next 60 seconds. If the RSI shows that an asset is oversold, you might consider buying a call option, expecting the price to rise in the next 60 seconds.

Hedging is another useful technique for beginners looking to minimize their risks. Hedging involves opening two opposite positions on the same asset at the same time. For example, you might buy a call option and a put option simultaneously. The idea is that no matter which direction the price moves, one of the options will generate profits that offset the losses of the other. This strategy can be especially useful in volatile markets where prices can change quickly. However, it is important to note that hedging can limit your potential profits, as losses on one option will reduce the profits on the other.

In addition to these strategies, it is essential to have a solid risk management plan. Risk management involves setting clear limits for your losses and profits and adhering to them strictly. A common rule in risk management is not to risk more than 1-2% of your total capital on a single trade. This will help you protect your capital and avoid significant losses. It is also important to diversify your investments and not put all your capital into a single trade or asset. Diversification can help you spread your risk and increase your chances of success in the long run.

Finally, it is crucial to keep a detailed record of all your trades. Keeping a log of your trades will allow you to analyze your performance, identify patterns, and adjust your strategies as needed. You can use a simple spreadsheet to record the date, asset, option type, amount invested, trade outcome, and any relevant comments or notes. Regularly reviewing your trading log will help you learn from your mistakes and improve your trading skills over time.

In summary, basic beginner strategies for binary options trading include trend following, breakouts, double reversal, 60 second strategy, and hedging. Each of these strategies has its own advantages and risks, and it is important to choose the one that best suits your trading style and risk tolerance. By combining these strategies with proper risk management and detailed logging of your trades, you will be better prepared to navigate the binary options market and increase your chances of success. Remember that trading is a skill that is developed over time and practice, so stay patient and committed to your continuous learning and improvement.

Advanced Strategies for Experienced Traders

Binary options trading may seem simple at first, but as you gain more experience and knowledge, it is essential to adopt more advanced strategies to maximize your profits and minimize risks. In this chapter, we will explore some advanced strategies designed for experienced traders. These strategies require a higher level of analysis and understanding of the market, but can offer significant rewards if implemented correctly.

One of the most commonly used advanced strategies is the advanced technical analysis strategy. This strategy involves using multiple technical indicators and chart patterns to make informed trading decisions. While beginners may rely on a single indicator such as the moving average, experienced traders combine multiple indicators to gain a more comprehensive view of the market. For example, you can use the relative strength index (RSI) along with the MACD (moving average convergence/divergence) and Bollinger bands to identify more accurate entry and exit points. Using multiple indicators can help you confirm trends and avoid false signals, thereby increasing your chances of success.

Another advanced strategy is the divergence strategy. Divergence occurs when the price of an asset moves in one direction while a technical indicator, such as the RSI or MACD, moves in the opposite direction. Divergence can be a powerful signal that a trend reversal is about to occur. For example, if the price of an asset is rising but the RSI is falling, this can indicate that the uptrend is losing steam and the price is likely to start falling. Experienced traders use divergence to identify trading opportunities before significant market changes occur.

The Fibonacci retracement strategy is another advanced technique that can be extremely useful. This strategy is based on the idea that asset prices tend to retrace to specific levels before continuing in the direction of the main trend. These levels are based on the Fibonacci sequence, which identifies key ratios, such as 38.2%, 50%, and 61.8%. By using Fibonacci retracement tools on price charts, you can identify these levels and look for trading opportunities. For example, if an asset price is in an uptrend and begins to retrace, you can use Fibonacci levels to identify potential bounce points where you could buy a call option. Similarly, in a downtrend, Fibonacci levels can help you identify resistance points where you could buy a put option.

The news trading strategy is another advanced technique that involves taking advantage of economic events and market news to make trades. Economic news, such as employment reports, interest rate decisions, and corporate earnings reports, can have a significant impact on asset prices. Experienced traders keep an eye on these events and use fundamental analysis to predict how they will affect the market. For example, if a jobs report is expected to be positive, you might anticipate a rise in the price of labor market-related assets and buy call options. However, it is important to note that news trading can be risky due to the volatility these events can cause. Therefore, it is crucial to have good risk management and be prepared to act quickly.

The correlation trading strategy involves analyzing the relationship between different assets and using this information to make trading decisions. Some assets tend to move in the same direction (positive correlation), while others move in opposite directions (negative correlation). By understanding these correlations, you can identify trading opportunities and diversify your portfolio to reduce risk. For example, if you notice that the price of gold and the US dollar have a negative correlation, you can take advantage of this relationship to trade in both directions. If the price of gold goes up, the dollar is likely to go down, and vice versa. Using the correlation strategy allows you to make more informed decisions and balance your risk in the market.

The ladder options trading strategy is another advanced technique that can offer huge profits. Ladder options are a type of binary option that offers multiple predetermined price levels (steps) with different payouts. Instead of simply predicting whether the price of an asset will go up or down, you can choose from several price levels and bet on which level you think the price will reach before expiration. This strategy allows you to diversify your investments and increase your chances of success by having more options to choose from. However, it also requires deeper analysis and a clear understanding of market movements.

The contrarian trading strategy is another advanced technique that involves trading against the current market trend. This strategy is based on the idea that trends do not last forever and will eventually reverse. Contrarian traders look for signs of exhaustion in the current trend and take positions in the opposite direction. For example, if the market is in a prolonged uptrend and you start to see signs of exhaustion, such as a decline in trading volume or the appearance of reversal patterns, you might consider buying a put option. This strategy can be risky, as trading against the main trend goes against conventional market wisdom. However, it can offer great rewards if executed correctly.

Finally, automated trading strategy is an advanced technique that involves using algorithms and trading robots to automatically execute trades based on predefined rules. This strategy allows you to remove emotions from trading and ensure that your trades are executed consistently and accurately. You can program your trading robots to follow a specific strategy, such as the trend following strategy or the Fibonacci retracement strategy, and let them perform trades on your behalf. However, it is crucial to test and fine-tune any automated strategy on a demo account before using it with real money to ensure that it works as you expect.

In summary, advanced strategies for experienced traders include advanced technical analysis, divergence, Fibonacci retracement, news trading, correlation, ladder options, contrarian trading, and automated trading. Each of these strategies requires a higher level of analysis and understanding of the market, but can offer significant rewards if implemented correctly. As you gain more experience and knowledge in binary options trading, it is critical to continue learning and adapting to changing market conditions. Remember that trading is a skill that is developed over time and practice, so stay patient and committed to your learning and continued improvement.

Technical Analysis in Binary Options

Technical analysis is a fundamental tool for any binary options trader. It relies on the study of historical data on the price and volume of an asset to predict future price movements. Unlike fundamental analysis, which focuses on economic and financial factors, technical analysis focuses exclusively on market behavior and price trends. In this chapter, we will explore the basics of technical analysis and how you can use it to improve your trading decisions.

Technical analysis is based on the premise that all the information needed to make trading decisions is already reflected in the price of an asset. This means that you don't need to analyze financial reports or economic news; instead, you just need to look at price charts and technical indicators. Price charts are visual representations of how the price of an asset has changed over time. The most common chart types are line charts, bar charts, and candlestick charts.

Candlestick charts are particularly popular among binary options traders because of the amount of information they provide. Each candle on the chart represents a specific time period, such as a minute, hour, or day. Candlesticks have bodies and shadows, which show the opening price, closing price, highest price, and lowest price during that period. Bullish candlesticks, which indicate an increase in price, are usually green or white, while bearish candlesticks, which indicate a decrease in price, are usually red or black.

One of the most important concepts in technical analysis is trend identification. A trend is the general direction in which the price of an asset is moving. Trends can be bullish, bearish, or sideways. An uptrend is characterized by a series of rising highs and lows, while a downtrend is characterized by a series of falling highs and lows. A sideways trend occurs when the price moves in a narrow range with no clear direction. Identifying the dominant trend is crucial because it allows you to align your trades with the direction of the market, which increases your chances of success.

To identify trends, traders use tools such as moving averages. A moving average is a technical indicator that shows the average price of an asset over a specific period of time. For example, a 50-day moving average calculates the average price of an asset over the past 50 days. Moving averages can be simple (SMA) or exponential (EMA). Simple moving averages weight all prices equally, while exponential moving averages give more weight to recent prices. When an asset's price is above its moving average, this indicates an uptrend, and when it is below it, it indicates a downtrend.

Another key concept in technical analysis is identifying support and resistance levels. Support is a price level where the demand for an asset is strong enough to stop a fall in price. In other words, it is a level where buyers tend to enter the market and push the price up. Resistance, on the other hand, is a level where the supply of an asset is strong enough to stop a rise in price. It is a level where sellers tend to enter the market and push the price down. Identifying these levels is crucial because they can act as reversal points where the price changes direction.

Technical indicators are mathematical tools that traders use to analyze market behavior and make trading decisions. Some of the most popular indicators are the Relative Strength Index (RSI), MACD (Moving Average Convergence/Divergence), and Bollinger Bands. The RSI is an oscillator that measures the speed and change of price movements. It moves in a range from 0 to 100 and is used to identify overbought and oversold conditions. When the RSI is above 70, the asset is overbought and the price is likely to fall. When the RSI is below 30, the asset is oversold and the price is likely to rise.

The MACD is another popular indicator that shows the relationship between two moving averages of different periods. It consists of the MACD line, the signal line, and the histogram. When the MACD line crosses above the signal line, this indicates a buy signal, and when it crosses below it, it indicates a sell signal. Bollinger Bands are another useful indicator that shows market volatility. They consist of an upper band, a lower band, and a central moving average. The bands expand and contract based on market volatility. When the price moves close to the upper band, this indicates that the asset is overbought, and when it moves close to the lower band, it indicates that the asset is oversold.

In addition to these indicators, chart patterns are an important part of technical analysis. Chart patterns are specific formations that are created by price movements and can predict future price movements. Some common patterns include the head and shoulders, triangles, and double tops and bottoms. For example, the head and shoulders pattern is a reversal signal that indicates that an uptrend is coming to an end and a downtrend is likely to begin. Recognizing these patterns can help you make more informed trading decisions.

In short, technical analysis is a powerful tool for binary options traders that relies on studying historical price and volume data to predict future price movements. By using candlestick charts, identifying trends, support and resistance levels, and applying technical indicators and chart patterns, you can significantly improve your trading decisions. Although technical analysis may seem complex at first, with practice and experience, it will become an essential part of your trading strategy. Always remember to combine technical analysis with good risk management to maximize your profits and minimize your losses.

Fundamental Analysis for Binary Options

Adrienne Morel

Fundamental analysis is an essential tool for binary options traders looking to understand and predict long-term market movements. Unlike technical analysis, which focuses on the study of charts and price patterns, fundamental analysis relies on the examination of economic, financial, and other qualitative and quantitative factors that can influence the value of an asset. In this chapter, we will explore the basics of fundamental analysis and how you can use it to improve your binary options trading decisions.

Fundamental analysis works from the premise that the value of an asset is influenced by a number of underlying factors that affect its supply and demand. These factors can be economic reports, corporate news, changes in government policy, geopolitical events, and many others. For example, if a company reports significantly higher than expected earnings, its stock price is likely to rise. Similarly, if a country experiences robust economic growth, its currency may strengthen relative to other currencies.

One of the most important aspects of fundamental analysis is monitoring economic indicators. These are data released by governments and other institutions that reflect the state of the economy. Some of the most relevant economic indicators include Gross Domestic Product (GDP), interest rates, inflation, unemployment, and retail sales. For example, an increase in GDP indicates that the economy is growing, which can lead to an increase in the value of that country's currency. On the other hand, a high unemployment rate can suggest a weak economy, which could devalue the currency.

Another key component of fundamental analysis is the study of interest rates. Interest rates are determined by central banks and have a significant impact on the economy and financial markets. When interest rates rise, borrowing becomes more expensive, which can slow economic growth. However, it can also attract investors seeking higher returns, which can strengthen the currency. Conversely, when interest rates fall, borrowing becomes cheaper, which can stimulate economic growth but can also lead to currency depreciation.

Inflation is another crucial factor in fundamental analysis. Inflation measures the overall increase in the prices of goods and services in an economy. Moderate inflation is generally seen as a sign of a healthy economy, but too high inflation can erode purchasing power and lead to an economic slowdown. Central banks closely monitor inflation and adjust interest rates to keep it at desirable levels. Therefore, binary options traders should keep an eye on inflation reports and central bank statements to anticipate movements in asset prices.

Corporate news and business events also play a major role in fundamental analysis. Earnings reports, mergers and acquisitions, management changes, and new products can significantly affect a company's stock price. For example, if a company announces an innovative new product that is expected to be successful in the market, its stock price is likely to rise. Similarly, if a company reports significant losses or faces legal problems, its stock price is likely to fall.

Geopolitical events and political decisions can also have a considerable impact on financial markets. Elections, trade policies, economic sanctions, and international conflicts can all influence the value of currencies, stocks, and other assets. For example, the imposition of trade tariffs between two countries can negatively affect companies that rely on international trade, which can lead to a drop in their stock price. Binary options traders should stay informed about geopolitical events and assess how they may affect the markets.

A useful tool in fundamental analysis is the economic calendar, which provides a list of important economic events and their release dates. These events include interest rate announcements, employment reports, inflation data, and much more. The economic calendar allows traders to be prepared for these events and adjust their trading strategies accordingly. For example, if a major interest rate announcement is expected from the Federal

Reserve, traders can anticipate increased volatility in the market and plan their trades accordingly.

It is important to mention that while fundamental analysis can provide valuable insight into the factors affecting the value of an asset, it is not always easy to predict how the market will react to these factors. Financial markets are complex and influenced by a multitude of interrelated variables. Therefore, it is useful to combine fundamental analysis with technical analysis to gain a more complete view of the market. While fundamental analysis tells you which assets have a solid underlying value, technical analysis helps you determine the best times to enter and exit the market.

In short, fundamental analysis is a powerful tool for binary options traders looking to understand and predict long-term market movements. By studying economic indicators, interest rates, inflation, corporate news, geopolitical events, and other relevant factors, you can make more informed trading decisions. Although it may seem overwhelming at first, with practice and dedication, fundamental analysis will become an integral part of your trading strategy. Always remember to stay informed and be prepared to adjust your trades in response to changes in the economic and political environment.

Risk Management in Binary Options

Risk management is one of the most important aspects of binary options trading. While it is exciting to invest and hope to make a profit, it is also crucial to recognize that trading involves significant risks. Without good risk management, it is easy to lose a considerable amount of money in a short period of time. In this chapter, we will explore the basic principles of risk management and how you can apply them to protect your capital and increase your chances of long-term success.

First, it's crucial to understand what risk management is. In simple terms, risk management is the process of identifying, assessing, and taking steps to reduce the risks associated with trading. This involves setting limits on how much you are willing to lose on a single trade, in a single day, or in a single week. It also involves diversifying your investments so that you don't put all your resources into one asset or strategy. Risk management doesn't guarantee that you'll never lose money, but it does help minimize losses and protect your capital.

One of the most important concepts in risk management is position sizing. This means deciding how much money you are going to invest in a single trade. A commonly recommended rule is to not risk more than 1% to 2% of your total capital on a single trade. For example, if you have a capital of $1,000, you should not risk more than $10 to $20 on a single trade. This way, even if you have a series of losing trades, you will not lose all of your capital quickly and you will have a chance to recover.

Another key aspect of risk management is the use of stop-loss and take-profit. A stop-loss is an order you place with your broker to sell an asset when it reaches a certain price. This helps you limit your losses in case the market moves against you. For example, if you buy a binary option expecting the price of an asset to rise, you can set a stop-loss at a lower price to limit your losses if the market falls. Similarly, a take-profit is an order you place to sell an asset when it reaches a certain price in your favor, locking in your profits. This helps you not to get too greedy and to take your profits when the market is in your favor.

Diversification is another essential principle in risk management. This means not putting all your money into one asset or type of binary option. Instead, you should spread your capital across different assets and strategies. For example, you can invest in different currency pairs, stocks, indices, and commodities. This way, if one asset doesn't perform as you expected, your other investments can make up for the losses. Diversification helps you reduce risk and increase your chances of long-term success.

Emotional control is also a crucial component of risk management. Trading can be emotionally challenging, especially when you are losing money. It is easy to get carried away by fear or greed and make impulsive decisions that can increase your losses. It is important to stay calm and stick to your trading plan, even when things are not going well. This means setting clear rules for when to enter and exit the market and sticking to them. It also means accepting that losses are part of trading and that the important thing is to stay in control and not let emotions dictate your decisions.

Education and continuous learning are essential for good risk management. The binary options market is constantly changing and it is important to stay informed about the latest trends and strategies. This involves reading books, taking courses, attending seminars and shadowing experienced traders. The more you know about the market and how it works, the better equipped you will be to manage risk and make informed decisions.

Another useful strategy is to keep a trading journal. This involves recording all of your trades, including the reasons why you entered each trade, the results, and what you learned from each experience. Keeping a journal helps you identify patterns in your trading behavior and learn from your mistakes. It also gives you a clear view of your performance and helps you improve your risk management strategies over time.

Patience and discipline are also crucial to risk management. It is important not to rush into trades and wait for the right opportunities. This means being patient and waiting for market conditions that align with your strategy. It also means being disciplined and sticking to your trading plan, even when it is tempting to deviate from it. Patience and discipline help you stay in control and avoid impulsive decisions that can increase your risks.

In summary, risk management is an essential part of binary options trading. It involves determining your position size, using stop-loss and take-profit, diversifying your investments, controlling your emotions, continually educating yourself, keeping a trading journal, and being patient and disciplined. By following these principles, you can protect your capital and increase your chances of long-term success. Although trading involves risks, good risk management helps you minimize them and maximize your chances of winning. Remember that the goal is not to avoid losses altogether, but to manage them in a way that allows you to continue trading and growing as a trader.

Trading Psychology

Trading psychology is an essential aspect that is often overlooked, but is crucial to success in the world of binary options trading. Beyond technical and fundamental analysis, emotional control and the right mindset play a vital role in decision making. In this chapter, we will explore how psychology influences your trading and how you can develop a strong and disciplined mindset to improve your results.

Trading can be an emotional roller coaster. Constant market fluctuations can trigger a wide range of emotions, from euphoria to panic. One of the most common emotions traders face is fear. Fear can arise from uncertainty about the market, fear of losing money, or anxiety about making wrong decisions. Fear can lead to paralysis, where you don't dare to make decisions, or to impulsive actions, where you make rash decisions without proper analysis.

Greed is another powerful emotion in trading. When the market is going in your favor and you are making money, it is easy to get carried away by greed and want to make more profit. Greed can lead to unwise decisions, such as not closing a winning trade at the right time or increasing your risk without a solid justification. Both scenarios can result in significant losses.

Hope is an emotion that can be both positive and negative. Hope can motivate you to keep going and maintain a positive attitude. However, it can also lead you to hold on to losing positions in the hope that the market will turn in your favor. It is important to balance hope with an objective assessment of the situation and be willing to accept losses when necessary.

Frustration is another common emotion in trading. Losses are inevitable, and every trader will experience setbacks at some point. Frustration can lead to a downward spiral, where you start making impulsive decisions to recoup losses, often resulting in more losses. It is crucial to learn how to manage frustration and stay calm and composed even during tough times.

One of the keys to managing these emotions is to have a clear trading plan and follow it rigorously. A trading plan defines your goals, strategies, entry and exit criteria, and risk limits. By having a well-defined plan, you reduce the influence of emotions on your decisions. Instead of reacting impulsively to market movements, you can follow your plan and make decisions based on objective criteria.

Discipline is key in trading psychology. Discipline involves following your trading plan without deviating, even when it is tempting to do so. This means resisting the temptation to increase your risk when you are winning or to hold onto losing positions in the hope of a reversal. Discipline helps you stay in control and avoid impulsive decisions that can damage your trading account.

Self-control is another essential skill for traders. Self-control involves the ability to regulate your emotions and behaviors, especially in high-pressure situations. This can include taking a break when you feel overwhelmed, avoiding trading when you are emotionally upset, and practicing relaxation techniques to stay calm. Self-control allows you to maintain an objective perspective and make rational decisions.

The right mindset is also crucial to trading success. This includes having a growth mindset, where you see losses as learning opportunities and are willing to constantly improve. Resilience is part of this mindset, allowing you to bounce back from losses and move forward with a positive attitude. It also involves accepting that losses are a natural part of trading and not allowing them to affect your confidence and motivation.

Trading also requires a great deal of patience. Markets won't always move in your favor, and it can take time for your strategies to pay off. Patience involves waiting for high-probability setups and not rushing into trades. It also means having the willingness to wait for the market to confirm your expectations before acting. Patience helps you avoid impulsive decisions and stay in control.

Stress management is another important part of trading psychology. Trading can be stressful, especially when you face losses or uncertainty in the market. Finding effective ways to manage stress, such as exercise, meditation, and setting work boundaries, can help you maintain a balanced and focused mindset. Reducing stress allows you to think clearly and make informed decisions.

Self-confidence is essential for trading success. Confidence allows you to make decisions with conviction and stick to your trading plan. However, it is important to balance confidence with humility. Overconfidence can lead to complacency and taking unnecessary risks. It is crucial to remain humble and always be willing to learn and adapt to changing market conditions.

Social support can also be beneficial for trading psychology. Connecting with other traders, whether through online communities, study groups, or mentors, can provide you with a support network and a source of learning. Sharing experiences and strategies with others can help you improve your skills and stay motivated. Additionally, having a support system can help you keep perspective and better manage negative emotions.

In short, trading psychology is a critical component to success in the world of binary options trading. Managing your emotions, developing a disciplined and patient mindset, and maintaining a balanced perspective will help you make informed decisions and improve your results. As with any other skill, trading psychology requires practice and dedication. By working on these aspects, you can become a more effective and resilient trader, able to face market challenges with confidence and control.

Common Mistakes and How to Avoid Them

In the world of binary options trading, it's easy to make mistakes, especially if you're a beginner. These mistakes can cost you money and, worse, they can dampen your enthusiasm for continuing to learn and improve. However, by identifying these mistakes and learning how to avoid them, you can increase your chances of success. In this chapter, we'll discuss some of the most common mistakes traders make and how you can avoid them to protect your capital and improve your results.

One of the most common mistakes is not having a clear trading plan. Many beginner traders jump into the market without a clear strategy, leaving them at the mercy of their emotions and impulsive decisions. A trading plan should include your goals, criteria for entering and exiting trades, and risk limits. Without a plan, it's easy to get carried away by greed or fear, which can lead to significant losses. To avoid this mistake, take the time to develop and follow a well-thought-out trading plan.

Another common mistake is not managing risk properly. Risking a large portion of your capital on a single trade is a recipe for disaster. A general rule of thumb is to not risk more than 1% to 2% of your total capital on any single trade. This means that even if you have a series of losing trades, you won't lose all of your capital. To avoid this mistake, set clear limits on how much you're willing to risk and stick to them strictly.

Excessive trading, or "overtrading," is another common mistake. Overtrading occurs when you make too many trades in a short period of time, often driven by emotion or impatience. This behavior can increase your transaction costs and risk of losses. It's important to be selective and wait for high-probability opportunities rather than trading on every small market move. To avoid overtrading, define clear criteria for your trades and follow your trading plan without deviation.

Emotional trading is another big mistake. Emotions such as fear, greed, hope, and frustration can influence your trading decisions and lead you to make mistakes. For example, fear can cause you to close winning trades too early, while greed can lead you to hold onto losing positions in the hope of a reversal. To avoid this mistake, it is crucial to stay calm and stick to your trading plan, regardless of the emotions you are feeling at the moment.

Lack of education and preparation is another common mistake. Binary options trading requires a solid understanding of the markets, strategies, and tools available. Many beginner traders do not spend enough time educating themselves before they begin trading. It is crucial to read books, take courses, practice with demo accounts, and learn from experienced traders. The more prepared you are, the better you will be able to make informed decisions and avoid costly mistakes.

Another mistake traders make is not diversifying their investments. Putting all your capital into a single asset or strategy can be very risky. Diversification allows you to spread risk across different assets and strategies, which can help protect your capital in case a trade doesn't go as you expected. To avoid this mistake, make sure you diversify your portfolio and don't rely on just one source of income.

Lack of discipline is another common problem. Discipline involves following your trading plan and risk management rules without deviating, even when it is tempting to do so. Without discipline, it is easy to fall into impulsive trading and make decisions based on emotions rather than rational analysis. To avoid this mistake, work on developing and maintaining strong discipline in your daily trading.

Not using stop-loss is a critical mistake. A stop-loss is a tool that allows you to set a loss limit for each trade. If the market moves against you, the stop-loss will close the trade automatically to limit your losses. Many beginner traders do not use stop-loss, which can lead to catastrophic losses. To avoid this mistake, always use stop-loss on your trades and adjust the levels according to your risk management strategy.

Irrational hope is another mistake that plagues many traders. Holding onto a losing position in the hope that the market will turn around can be detrimental. Instead of accepting the loss and learning from the experience, some traders continue to hope for a turnaround that may not come. To avoid this mistake, accept that losses are part of trading and don't let irrational hope influence your decisions.

Failing to review and learn from your trades is another common mistake. Failing to analyze your past trades can lead you to repeat the same mistakes over and over again. Keeping a trading journal where you record all your trades, the reasons behind them, and the results, allows you to identify patterns and learn from your mistakes. To avoid this mistake, make it a habit to regularly review your trading journal and adjust your strategies as needed.

Finally, a common mistake is not having patience. Successful trading is not about making money quickly, but about being consistent and patient over time. Impatience can lead you to make hasty and risky decisions. To avoid this mistake, keep a long-term perspective and be patient, waiting for the right opportunities to enter the market.

In short, making mistakes is part of the learning process in binary options trading, but many of these mistakes can be avoided with proper preparation and a disciplined mindset. Having a clear trading plan, properly managing risk, avoiding overtrading, controlling emotions, continually educating yourself, diversifying investments, maintaining discipline, using stop-losses, avoiding irrational hope, reviewing and learning from trades, and being patient are key principles to avoiding common mistakes and increasing your chances of success. By focusing on these aspects, you can protect your capital, improve your results, and build a stronger, more sustainable trading career.

Developing Your Trading Plan

Developing a solid trading plan is one of the most important steps for any trader, whether you are a beginner or an experienced trader. A trading plan is essentially your roadmap for trading the market. It includes your goals, strategies, criteria for entering and exiting trades, and how you are going to manage risk. Having a plan helps you maintain discipline, avoid impulsive decisions, and increase your chances of success. In this chapter, we will explain how to develop a trading plan in a simple and straightforward manner, making sure that it is easy to understand and implement.

The first step in developing your trading plan is to define your goals. Think about what you want to achieve from binary options trading. Are you looking to generate additional income, build a primary source of income, or simply learn and improve your skills? Your goals should be specific, measurable, attainable, relevant, and time-bound. For example, you could set a goal like "Earn a 10% return on my investment in the next six months." Having clear goals will give you direction and help you measure your progress.

Once you have your goals clear, the next step is to define your trading strategy. The trading strategy is the set of rules and criteria that you will follow to make buying and selling decisions. There are many different strategies that you can use in binary options trading, from trend-based strategies to news-based strategies. The important thing is to choose a strategy that suits your trading style and goals. Research different strategies, test some of them on a demo account, and choose the one that works best for you.

After defining your strategy, you need to set your criteria for entering and exiting trades. These criteria should be clear and specific so that you know exactly when you should open or close a position. For example, you might decide to enter a trade when the price of an asset crosses above a 50-day moving average, and exit when it crosses below a 20-day moving average. Having specific criteria will help you avoid impulsive decisions and stay focused on your strategy.

Risk management is another critical component of your trading plan. You need to define how much you are willing to risk on each trade and how you are going to manage your losses. A common rule of thumb is to not risk more than 1% to 2% of your total capital on a single trade. This protects you from large losses and allows you to stay in the game for the long term. Additionally, it is important to use tools such as stop-losses to limit your losses and protect your capital. A stop-loss is an order that automatically closes your trade if the market moves against you, thus limiting your losses.

Another important aspect of your trading plan is how you're going to manage your profits. It's tempting to let profits continue to grow, but it's also important to know when to take profits to lock them in. You could set profit targets, such as closing a trade when you've made a 5% or 10% return. You could also use take-profit orders, which automatically close your trade when the price reaches a predetermined level.

Managing your profits will help you keep your results consistent and avoid losing what you've already made.

Your trading plan should also include a daily trading routine. This includes when and how you will analyze the market, when you will place your trades, and how you will record your results. Having a daily routine helps you maintain discipline and ensure that you are consistently following your plan. For example, you might decide to check the markets every morning before you start trading, place your trades between 10 a.m. and 12 a.m., and review your results at the end of the day.

Logging your trades is another essential component of your trading plan. Keeping a detailed record of all your trades allows you to analyze your performance, identify patterns, and learn from your mistakes. Your log should include details such as the date and time of the trade, the asset, the entry and exit price, the position size, the outcome of the trade, and any observations or comments. Reviewing your logs regularly will help you improve your strategy and make more informed decisions.

Finally, your trading plan should include a section on how you are going to evaluate and adjust your plan. The binary options market is dynamic and ever-changing, so it is important to review and adjust your plan regularly to ensure that it remains effective. You could set up a schedule to review your plan every month or every quarter and make adjustments as needed. This will allow you to adapt to changing market conditions and continually improve your trading approach.

In summary, developing a solid trading plan is critical to success in binary options trading. Your plan should include your goals, your trading strategy, your criteria for entering and exiting trades, how you will manage risk and profit, your daily trading routine, how you will record your trades, and how you will evaluate and adjust your plan. By following a well-defined trading plan, you can maintain discipline, avoid impulsive decisions, and increase your chances of success in the binary options market.

Case Studies and Real Examples

Case studies and real-life examples are a powerful tool for understanding how binary options trading works in practice. By analyzing concrete situations and seeing how strategies are applied in the real world, you can gain a deeper understanding of the challenges and opportunities you will face as a trader. In this chapter, we will present you with some case studies and real-life examples that illustrate how to apply key concepts of binary options trading, how to manage risk, and how to learn from mistakes to improve your results.

Let's imagine the case of John, a novice trader who has decided to try his luck in binary options trading. John starts with a demo account to familiarize himself with the platform and test different strategies without risking his real money. After a few weeks of practice, John feels ready to trade with real money. His goal is to generate a monthly return of 5% on his initial investment of $1,000.

John has read about the price action trading strategy, which involves analyzing patterns in an asset's price movements to make trading decisions. He decides to try this strategy on the EUR/USD currency pair, which is one of the most popular and liquid pairs on the binary options market. John sets a clear rule for his strategy: he will open a buy trade when the EUR/USD price crosses above a 50-period moving average and a sell trade when it crosses below it.

In his first week, John sees a buying opportunity when the EUR/USD price crosses above the 50-period moving average. He decides to invest $50 in a call option with a one-hour expiry. At the end of the hour, the EUR/USD price has risen and John makes a profit of 80% on his investment, or $40. Encouraged by this success, John continues to apply his strategy for the rest of the week and manages to win three more similar trades, accumulating a total of $160 in profit.

However, in the second week, John faces a series of losing trades. The EUR/USD price is more volatile than usual and John loses three trades in a row, each worth $50. Instead of getting discouraged, John decides to analyze his trades to understand what went wrong. He realizes that he failed to account for important economic events that affected market volatility, such as the release of US employment data. Learning from his mistakes, John adjusts his trading plan to include analysis of important economic events before opening new trades.

In the third week, John implements his improved strategy and wins two trades in a row again, recovering part of his losses. Over the next few months, John continues to adjust and improve his trading plan, and although he has ups and downs, he manages to achieve his goal of generating a 5% monthly return on his initial investment. This case study shows how discipline, adaptation, and continuous learning are key to success in binary options trading.

Now let's look at the case of Anna, a more experienced trader who specializes in news-based trading strategy. Anna focuses on important economic events that can cause significant movements in asset prices. Her trading plan includes a detailed economic calendar and clear rules for trading before and after the release of economic data.

One day, Anna sees that the monthly US employment report, known as Non-Farm Payrolls (NFP), is about to be released. This report usually causes a lot of volatility in the currency market, especially in pairs that include the US dollar. Anna decides to trade the USD/JPY pair based on the outcome of the report. Her rule is to wait for the report to be released and then observe the initial market reaction.

When the report is released, it shows a larger than expected increase in employment, which is typically positive for the dollar. Anna notices that the price of USD/JPY rises rapidly in response to the news. She decides to invest $100 in a call option with a 30-minute expiration. At the end of 30 minutes, the price of USD/JPY has risen even further, and Anna has made a profit of 70%, or $70.

Over the next few months, Ana continues to apply her news-based strategy and consistently manages to generate profits. However, she also faces challenges. On one occasion, she decides to trade based on an inflation report that turns out to be less impactful than expected, and her trade results in a loss. Ana learns that not all economic events have the same impact and adjusts her trading plan to be more selective in the news she chooses to trade.

These case studies of John and Anna illustrate different approaches to binary options trading and highlight the importance of having a clear trading plan, managing risk and learning from experiences. John shows how price action strategy can be effective if applied with discipline and adjusted according to market conditions. Anna, on the other hand, demonstrates how a news-based strategy can generate significant profits if done with proper research and analysis.

When looking at these real-life examples, it is important to remember that binary options trading is not without risk. Successful traders are those who are willing to learn from their mistakes, adjust their strategies, and maintain discipline at all times. Whether you prefer price action, technical analysis, fundamental analysis, or a combination of these approaches, the crucial thing is to develop a trading plan that suits your style and goals, and to follow it consistently.

In short, case studies and real-life examples are an invaluable tool for understanding how to apply binary options trading strategies in practice. By learning from other traders' experiences, you can avoid common mistakes, improve your skills, and increase your chances of success. Whether you're just starting out in binary options trading or looking to improve your results, studying real-life cases will provide you with valuable lessons and help you develop a more solid and effective trading approach.

Adrienne Morel

Innovations and Trends in Binary Options

The world of binary options trading is constantly evolving. Technological innovations and emerging trends are transforming the way traders interact with the financial markets. Keeping up with these innovations and trends is crucial for any trader who wants to stay competitive and maximize their chances of success. In this chapter, we will explore some of the major innovations and trends in binary options trading, highlighting how they can benefit you and what you should keep in mind to make the most of them.

One of the most significant innovations in binary options trading is automation. Trading robots and automated systems have gained popularity in recent years. These systems use advanced algorithms to analyze the market and execute trades on behalf of the trader. The main advantage of automation is that it removes emotions from the trading process, which can lead to more rational and consistent decisions. In addition, trading robots can operate around the clock, making it possible to take advantage of opportunities that could arise at any time, even when the trader is sleeping or busy with other activities.

However, it is important to remember that not all trading robots are created equal. Some are better designed than others and offer more reliable results. Before relying on an automated system, it is crucial to research and test its performance on a demo account. This will allow you to evaluate its effectiveness without risking your real money. Additionally, it is advisable to use trading robots as a complementary tool rather than relying on them entirely. Maintaining active monitoring and making adjustments as needed is essential to maximizing the benefits of automation.

Another important trend in binary options trading is the increasing integration of trading platforms with mobile devices. Mobile trading apps allow traders to access the markets and execute trades from their smartphones or tablets. This flexibility is especially valuable in today's world, where mobility and quick response are key. With a mobile trading app, you can monitor your positions, receive market alerts, and place trades on the go, allowing you to react quickly to opportunities or risks that may arise.

Artificial intelligence technology and machine learning are also making their mark on binary options trading. These technologies can analyze large amounts of data and recognize patterns that might not be apparent to the human eye. By using AI for market analysis, traders can gain more accurate and detailed insights, which can improve decision making. For example, an AI system could analyze financial news, economic data, and price movements to predict the future direction of an asset.

However, as with automation, it is important to use AI as a complementary tool. Human oversight remains crucial to correctly interpreting data and making informed decisions. AI can provide a competitive advantage, but it should not completely replace human judgment in the trading process.

Blockchain technology and cryptocurrencies are also influencing the world of binary options trading. Blockchain technology provides greater transparency and security in transactions, which can be beneficial for traders. Some binary options trading platforms have started accepting cryptocurrencies as a form of payment, offering an additional alternative for traders who prefer to use digital assets. Additionally, cryptocurrency-based binary options are gaining popularity, allowing traders to speculate on the price direction of cryptocurrencies such as Bitcoin, Ethereum, and others.

In addition to technological innovations, regulatory trends are also affecting binary options trading. In recent years, many countries have implemented stricter regulations to protect traders from fraudulent practices and ensure a safer and fairer trading environment. These regulations include licensing requirements for brokers, transparency in reporting, and the implementation of measures to prevent fraud. It is critical for traders to choose brokers that comply with relevant regulations and operate transparently and responsibly.

Social media and online communities are also playing a major role in binary options trading. Platforms such as Twitter, Reddit and specialized forums allow traders to share information, strategies and experiences. These communities can be a valuable source of learning and support, especially for beginner traders. However, it is important to be critical and verify information before making decisions based on recommendations from other traders. Not all strategies or advice found online are reliable, and it is essential to do your own research and analysis.

Another emerging trend is social trading, which allows traders to copy the trades of experienced traders. Some trading platforms offer copy trading features, where you can view other traders' trading history and choose to copy their strategies. This trend is especially appealing to beginners who want to learn by watching more experienced traders. However, as with any trading strategy, it is important to do thorough research and understand the risks before following other traders.

In short, innovations and trends in binary options trading are transforming the way traders interact with financial markets. From automation and mobile apps to artificial intelligence, blockchain technology, and social trading, these innovations offer new opportunities and challenges. Keeping up with these trends and adapting to changes is crucial to succeeding in the world of binary options trading. By using these tools in a smart and complementary way, you can improve your trading skills and increase your chances of success in this exciting and dynamic market.

Conclusions and Final Reflections

Throughout this book, we have explored the world of binary options trading from its basic fundamentals to the most advanced strategies and the latest technological innovations. Now, it is time to reflect on everything we have learned and highlight the most important takeaways that you can take with you as you move forward on your trading journey.

First and foremost, it is crucial to remember that binary options trading, like any other form of investment, involves risks. The prospect of quick profits is appealing, but it must always be balanced with a clear understanding of the risks involved. Success in trading is not just about making correct predictions, but also about managing those risks effectively. Risk management is therefore not simply one aspect of trading, but its cornerstone. Setting loss limits, diversifying your investments, and not risking more than you can afford to lose are essential principles that should guide all your trading decisions.

Furthermore, trading psychology is a determining factor in your success or failure.

Emotions, such as fear and greed, can cloud your judgment and lead you to make impulsive decisions. Throughout this book, we have stressed the importance of maintaining a clear and objective mind. Developing the discipline to follow your trading plan, even when the market does not behave as you expected, is a crucial skill that can make the difference between success and failure. Always remember that trading is a marathon, not a sprint. Stay calm, keep learning, and continually improve your skills and strategies.

We have discussed the various strategies you can use, from the most basic to the most advanced. Each strategy has its place and can be effective in different market contexts. The key is to find the strategies that best suit your trading style and financial goals. There is no magic formula for success, but with patience, practice, and constant evaluation of your results, you can find the approach that works best for you.

Technical and fundamental analysis are essential tools in your trading arsenal. Technical analysis allows you to interpret market movements through charts and price patterns, while fundamental analysis helps you understand the underlying economic forces driving those movements. Using both forms of analysis in a complementary way will give you a more complete view of the market and allow you to make more informed decisions.

Choosing a suitable trading platform is another crucial aspect we have covered. The platform you choose should be reliable, easy to use, and offer all the tools needed to execute your strategies effectively. Do your research before settling on a platform and make sure it meets your specific trading needs.

As for innovations and trends, we have seen how automation, mobile apps, artificial intelligence, and blockchain technology are transforming binary options trading. Keeping up with these innovations and adapting to technological changes can give you a competitive edge in the market. Don't be afraid to try new tools and approaches, but always do so with caution and after proper research.

Finally, let's reflect on the importance of continuing education. The world of trading is dynamic and constantly evolving. Strategies that work today may not be effective tomorrow, and new opportunities and challenges can arise at any time. Commit to continuing to learn and improve your skills. Read books, participate in webinars, follow market news, and most importantly, learn from your own trading experiences. Every trade, whether winning or losing, is an opportunity to learn and grow as a trader.

In short, success in binary options trading does not happen overnight. It requires a combination of knowledge, skills, discipline and careful risk management. Stay focused on your goals, keep improving continuously and do not get carried away by emotions. With time and dedication, you can develop the skills necessary to succeed in this exciting and challenging field. We hope that this book has provided you with a solid foundation and has inspired you to continue forward on your trading path. Good luck and happy trading!

Adrienne Morel

www.ingramcontent.com/pod-product-compliance
Lightning Source LLC
Chambersburg PA
CBHW021114130726
47988CB00003B/1015